Teddy Bears' Christmas

Teddy Bears' Christmas

Holiday Greetings from
the Secret World of Teddy Bears

Photographs by Elaine Faris Keenan
Written by Pamela Prince
Designed and Illustrated by Ken Sansone

Harmony Books / New York

*The authors wish to thank Terence and Barbara Flynn,
and Carol Hacker, for their help and support.*

*Our warm appreciation to Doris Edgemon and to
Cami Edgemon Noble.*

*Our thanks to Heirloom Bears, Bev Wright and Lynda Carswell
designers, Woodside, California. Heirloom Bears appear on pages 13,
28-29, and 45. Heirloom Bears Copyright © 1981 by Beverly Wright
and Lynda Carswell.*

———————

*Photographs copyright © 1985 by Elaine Faris Keenan
Text copyright © 1985 by Pamela Prince
Silhouette illustrations copyright © 1985 by Ken Sansone*

*Published by Harmony Books, a division of Crown Publishers, Inc.,
One Park Avenue, New York, New York 10016 and simultaneously
in Canada by General Publishing Company Limited*

HARMONY and colophon are trademarks of Crown Publishers, Inc.

Manufactured in Japan

———————

Library of Congress Cataloging in Publication Data

*Prince, Pamela.
Teddy bears' Christmas.*

*Summary: Poems and photographs bring the teddy bears'
celebration of Christmas to us, revealing their preparations,
Santa's visit, and their enjoyment of the gifts.*
*1. Teddy bears—Juvenile poetry. 2. Christmas—Juvenile
poetry. 3. Children's poetry, American. [1. Teddy
bears—Poetry. 2. Toys—Poetry. 3. Christmas—Poetry.
4. American poetry] I. Keenan, Elaine Faris, ill. II. Sansone,
Ken, ill. III. Title.*
PS3566.R573T4 1985 811'.54 85-5454
ISBN: 0-517-55671-5

10 9 8 7 6 5 4 3 2 1

First Edition

———————

For Christopher and Andrew,
and for Ramona and Susan

I made my list, dear Santa, see!
I thought of others, not just me.
I put down things for Mom and Dad,
And it's been weeks since I've been bad.
I'll be so good the whole year through;
You must believe me, for it's true.
I promise I'll no longer tease
My cousin Ted, if only, please,
You think that maybe I could get
A speedy, silver new train set.
When we sing our Christmas carols
I won't giggle if some barrels
Of honey could be by the tree
On Christmas Day, just two or three.
I hope I get a little sled
All painted in a snappy red.
A pony would be very fine;
Imagine! It would be all mine . . .
Well, Santa, see what you can do.
Oh yes, and Merry Christmas, too!

Jerome writes his Christmas list

*L*it by the lamplight's friendly glow
Under a mantle of gentle snow,
A joyful sound! A Teddy trio,
Singing out tonight, *con brio.*
The three stay in tune, without a piano,
But they would be pleased to find a soprano
Who'd sing with them there in the crisp frosty air.
Let them know if you know of some sweet Teddy bear
Who'd be happy to join them and lend her high voice
To the music they make. Oh, just hear them rejoice
As their harmonies carry across the clear night,
And they wish you a holiday filled with delight!

Basil, Martin, and Malcolm
go Christmas caroling

*F*rederick and Howard and Cousin Sergei
Are performing at school in a play.
Family and friends will be happy to learn
What occurred on that first Christmas Day.
Howard has stage fright. "I wish that I were
Almost anywhere else; I would surely prefer
Not to be wearing this hat and this cape
With this pillow and package of myrrh."
Serge, in his turban, and Fred, to the right,
Feel so honored to stand here tonight.
They wait for their cue; they sing of the child
And the star filled with wonder and light.

Howard, Frederick, and Cousin Sergei play the Magi
bearing gifts in the holiday pageant at school

Eugene is staying home tonight,
Busy wrapping gifts by candlelight.
Christmas is just one day away,
There's lots to do for the holiday.
Inside the smallest box he wrapped
A bracelet for his sister, Pat;
And there's a book for Ned, his pal;
And cuff links for his Uncle Hal.
The present he now ties string around
Is a special one that he has found
To give a pretty little bear
With soft brown eyes whose name is Claire.
Eugene thinks she's the sweetest thing;
He'd love to give her everything.
But he picked out a pretty pot
Of golden honey and he bought
A silver spoon with which she'll eat
This lovingly chosen, special treat.
"It's fun to give, fun to receive,"
Thinks Eugene, on this Christmas Eve.

Eugene wraps his Christmas gifts

Frederick takes off this afternoon
To his Aunt Betty's home.
There he'll visit with his cousins
Randolph and Jerome.
He takes the presents Mama made—
They're stuffed snug in his pack.
He hopes his aunt will have some gifts
For him to carry back.
So now you see him, on his way;
He's headed for the town.
There's lots for him to do today
Before the sun goes down.

Frederick skis off to deliver
some Christmas presents

Through the forest tramped the three,

Looking for a perfect tree.

Bernice complained, "They're all too tall..."

And Frederick sighed, "...or way too small."

Eugene spied one, "Hey, I like that!"

But Fred replied, "It's awfully fat.

We'd never squeeze it down the hall;

It'd leave bad scratches on our wall."

Just when they feared they'd never find

An ideal tree, they looked behind

A little glade of snowy white,

And there it stood, completely right!

"We found it! Oh, it's grand! It's great!

Let's bring it back to decorate!"

Frederick, Eugene, and Bernice
bring home the Christmas tree

The Christmas tree looks bright and fine
All strung with shining beads,
Tiny presents and ornaments . . .
There's just one thing it needs.
Randolph gives his friend a lift.
The top seems very far.
Jerome holds up the sparkling,
Dazzling, silver star.

Randolph and Jerome give the Christmas tree
a finishing touch

T was the night before Christmas..." Mama Bear reads
To her two little bears dressed for bed.
Frederick's in green, and his sister, Irene,
Wears a nightgown and cap of bright red.
They're very excited. Tomorrow's the day!
Each time when the name *Santa Claus*
Is read aloud in the story, they shout
And clap with their four tiny paws.
The tea kettle's on, and they're feeling quite snug.
The fireplace glows warm and light.
"Merry Christmas to all..." so the story concludes
"And to all," Mama says, "a good night!"

Mama reads "'Twas the Night Before Christmas"
to Frederick and Irene on Christmas Eve

Down the chimney Santa tumbles
With his pack of toys,
Filling stockings, leaving presents
For the girls and boys.
Ned and Ed are tiny twins.
Among their Christmas treats
Are warm slippers by the hearth,
So cozy for their feet.
Sue's been good the whole year through;
Twice only was she naughty.
She's been asking for a pet,
A sprightly little Scottie!

Merry Christmas and Ho! Ho! Ho!

Nigel's glad it's Christmas morning.

At last he gets to peek

Inside the gift beneath the tree

He's eyed each day this week.

On Monday he picked up the box

And shook it left and right.

On Tuesday he snuck out of bed

And watched it most the night.

"What could it be?" he asked Bernice

On Wednesday afternoon.

On Thursday she said, "I won't tell;

You'll find out very soon."

He made a guess at three o'clock

On Friday; then by four

He'd changed his mind, and then by five

He'd made six guesses more.

Saturday, it was Christmas Eve,

And Nigel said a prayer.

"If I receive the toy I want

I'll be a Teddy bear

Who's good as gold the whole year through . . ."

And now the moment's here . . .

When Nigel spies what is inside

He gives a hearty cheer.

"My dream came true! My secret wish!

Hip, hip hooray! Oh, yes!"

Do *you* know what his gift could be?

Go on now, take a guess . . .

At last, Nigel gets to open his Christmas presents!

Teddy wonders "Who is this?
He hasn't any fur.
He's shiny and he never growls,
His only sound is *whirrr*...
He doesn't have my kind of eyes
But, still, he seems to see.
Two flashing lights are on his head
Where his two ears should be.
He's orange and red and silver;
His feet extremely green...
I think that he's the oddest fellow
That I have ever seen!"

Teddy isn't quite sure what to make of the new robot
underneath the Christmas tree

Howard had one thing in mind
When Christmas came this year.
His mama asked him what he'd like
From Santa and his reindeer.
"Would you like a woolen scarf?
Perhaps a paisley tie?
How about a bicycle
Or fresh-baked honey pie?"
Howard answered "Oh, no, no.
Please keep all of that stuff.
A nutcracker is what I want.
He'd be more than enough.
The kind who wears a handsome suit
That's painted white and red,
With boots and shiny buttons
And a helmet for his head.
His mouth and teeth are very strong
And when they start to shut
I'm glad that I'm a Teddy bear
And not some type of nut."
So here they are beneath the tree.
They're posing side by side:
A dapper soldier and a bear
Who's pleased and filled with pride.

Howard is very proud to pose
with the new Christmas nutcracker

Nicky's in a festive mood
And dressed up a special way;
Sporting cheerful winter pants
And cap knit by Aunt Fay.
Mama tied a ribbon 'round
His neck and added holly.
He certainly is looking fine
And feeling oh-so-jolly.
Underneath the tree he found
A wonderful surprise,
The gift that he's been hoping for—
A sled that's just his size.

Nicky finds a wonderful surprise
beneath the tree

The lake froze over Friday night.

Bernice runs out to skate.

She loves to wear her little skirt

And do a figure eight.

"Come on, Eugene," she calls to him.

"Please join me on the ice.

We'll have such fun. Just take my hand—

You'll find it very nice."

He's feeling apprehensive;

He's never tried this sport.

Bernice makes it look easy, though;

He watches her cavort.

Plucking up his courage,

He comes up to her side

And holds onto her shoulder,

As the two begin to glide

Upon the glistening surface

Round and round they go:

Flashing silver skates and Teddies

In the winter snow.

Bernice and Eugene go skating

Bernice became distracted
When she saw a handsome bear.
She skated off to flirt with him.
It wasn't very fair!
Eugene began to wobble,
Then he slipped and took a tumble.
He wasn't hurt or even sore.
He just felt kind of humble.
Sitting there he thought, "It's silly.
No harm done, but, oh! I am chilly."

*Eugene falls while skating, but he will be
on his feet in a minute*

On Christmas Day these two go out
To play and joke and gaily shout
And tumble in the sparkling snow
As Roscoe calls out, "Ho! Ho! Ho!"
He pushes Bertie down the slope
And as Bert slides he yells, "I hope
Your holidays are filled with cheer,
And have the happiest New Year!"

Roscoe gives Bert a friendly push
down the hill

How sweet and clear the music rings

When Teddy plucks the golden strings.

Just hear him, as he hums aloud

While floating aloft on his fleecy cloud,

With harp and halo shining bright

And feathery wings so snowy white.

He likes to sing of cheer and joy

And sends to every girl and boy

A Christmas wish for fun, for mirth,

For love and hope and peace on Earth.

Can you hear the sweet music
Teddy is playing on his harp?